Brunswick, Georgia
April 18, 1875

— I am convinced that God meant this land for people to rest in, — not to work in. If we were so constituted that life could be an idyll, then this were the place of places for it: but being, as it is, the hottest of battles, — a man might as well expect to plan a campaign in a dream as to make anything like his best fight here . . .

— *Sidney Lanier*
(from a letter to Margaret Peacock)

# *The* MARSHES OF GLYNN

*Sidney Lanier*

*Photographic interpretation by*
*Mose Daniels*

HANNAU ROBINSON INC

Library of Congress Catalog Card Number: 72-106367
Copyright 1949 – Marie B. Whittle

Second Printing, 1969

# The Marshes of Glynn

Glooms of the live-oaks, beautiful-braided and woven
  With intricate shades of the vines that myriad-cloven
    Clamber the forks of the multiform boughs, —
      Emerald twilights, —
      Virginal shy lights,

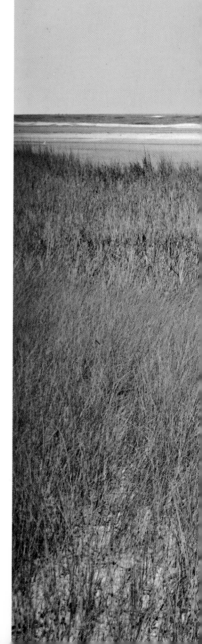

Wrought of the leaves to allure to the whisper of vows,
When lovers pace timidly down through the green colonnades
Of the dim sweet woods, of the dear dark woods,
   Of the heavenly woods and glades,
That run to the radiant marginal sand-beach within
   The wide sea-marshes of Glynn; —

Beautiful glooms, soft dusks in the noon-day fire, —
Wildwood privacies, closets of lone desire,
Chamber from chamber parted with wavering arras of leaves, —
Cells for the passionate pleasure of prayer to the soul that grieves, —
Pure with a sense of the passing of saints through the wood,
Cool for the dutiful weighing of ill with good; —

*O braided dusks of the oak and woven shades of the vine*
*While the riotous noon-day sun of the June-day long did shine*
*Ye held me fast in your heart and I held you fast in mine;*
*But now when the noon is no more, and riot is rest,*
*And the sun is a-wait at the ponderous gate of the West,*

*And the slant yellow beam down the wood-aisle doth seem*
*Like a lane into heaven that leads from a dream, —*

Aye, now, when my soul all day hath drunken the soul of the oak.
And my heart is at ease from men, and the wearisome sound of the stroke
Of the scythe of time and the trowel of trade is low,
And belief overmasters doubt, and I know that I know,
And my spirit is grown to a lordly great compass within,

That the length and the breadth and the sweep of the marshes of Glynn
Will work me no fear like the fear they have wrought me of yore
When length was fatigue, and when breadth was but bitterness sore,
And when terror and shrinking and dreary unnamable pain
Drew over me out of the merciless miles of the plain, —

*Oh, now, unafraid, I am fain to face*
*The vast sweet visage of space.*
*To the edge of the wood I am drawn, I am drawn,*

Where the gray beach glimmering runs, as a belt of the dawn,
   For a mete and a mark
     To the forest-dark: —
      So:
Affable live-oak, leaning low, —
Thus — with your favor — soft, with a reverent hand,
(Not lightly touching your person, Lord of the land!)
Bending your beauty aside, with a step I stand
On the firm-packed sand,

*Free*
*By a world of marsh that borders a world of sea.*

Sinuous southward and sinuous northward the shimmering band
Of the sand-beach fastens the fringe of the marsh to the folds
     of the land.

Inward and outward to northward and southward the beach-lines
     linger and curl
As a silver-wrought garment that clings to and follows the firm
     sweet limbs of a girl.
Vanishing, swerving, evermore curving again into sight,
Softly the sand-beach wavers away to a dim gray looping of light.

*And what if behind me to westward the wall of the woods stands
      high?
The world lies east: how ample, the marsh and the sea and the sky!*

A league and a league of marsh-grass, waist-high, broad in the blade,
Green, and all of a height, and unflecked with a light or a shade,
Stretch leisurely off, in a pleasant plain,
To the terminal blue of the main.

Oh, what is abroad in the marsh and the terminal sea?
Somehow my soul seems suddenly free
From the weighing of fate and the sad discussion of sin,
By the length and the breadth and the sweep of the marshes of Glynn.

Ye marshes, how candid and simple and nothing-withholding and free
Ye publish yourself to the sky and offer yourselves to the sea!

Tolerant plains, that suffer the sea and the rains and the sun,
Ye spread and span like the catholic man who hath mightily won
God out of knowledge and good out of infinite pain
And sight out of blindness and purity out of a stain.

*As the marsh-hen secretly builds on the watery sod,*
*Behold I will build me a nest on the greatness of God:*

*I will fly in the greatness of God as the marsh-hen flies*
*In the freedom that fills all the space 'twixt the marsh and the skies;*

*By so many roots as the marsh-grass sends in the sod*
*I will heartily lay me a-hold on the greatness of God:*

*Oh, like to the greatness of God is the greatness within*
*The range of the marshes, the liberal marshes of Glynn.*

And the sea lends large, as the marsh: lo, out of his plenty the sea
Pours fast: full soon the time of the flood-tide must be;

Look how the grace of the sea doth go
About and about through the intricate channels that flow
      Here and there,
        Everywhere,
Till his waters have flooded the uttermost creeks and the low-lying lanes,
And the marsh is meshed with a million veins,
That like as with rosy and silvery essences flow
  In the rose-and-silver evening glow.

*Farewell, my lord Sun!*

The creeks overflow: a thousand rivulets run
'Twixt the roots of the sod; the blades of the marsh-grass stir;
Passeth a hurrying sound of wings that westward whirr;

Passeth, and all is still; and the currents cease to run;
And the sea and the marsh are one.

How still the plains of the waters be!
The tide is in his ecstasy.
The tide is at his highest height:
       And it is night.

And now from the Vast of the Lord will the waters of sleep
Roll in on the souls of men,
But who will reveal to our waking ken
The forms that swim and the shapes that creep
       Under the waters of sleep?
And I would I could know what swimmeth below when the tide comes in
On the length and the breadth of the marvelous marshes of Glynn.